DEINONYCHUS

Titles in the Dinosaur Profiles series include:

DINOSAUR PROFILES

DEINONYCHUS

Text by Fabio Marco Dalla Vecchia
Illustrations by Leonello Calvetti and Luca Massini

BLACKBIRCH®
PRESS

THOMSON
GALE

San Diego • Detroit • New York • San Francisco • Cleveland • New Haven, Conn. • Waterville, Maine • London • Munich

Computer illustrations 3D and 2D: Leonello Calvetti and Luca Massini

Photographs: pages 22–23 Louie Psihoyos/Grazia Neri

LIBRARY OF CONGRESS CATALOGING-IN-PUBLICATION DATA

Dalla Vecchia, Fabio Marco.
  Deinonychus / text by Fabio Marco Dalla Vecchia; illustrations by Leonello Calvetti and Luca Massini.
     p. cm. — (Dinosaur profiles)
  Includes bibliographical references and index.
  ISBN 1-4103-0498-1 (paperback : alk. paper)
  ISBN 1-4103-0328-4 (hardback : alk. paper)
  1. Deinonychus—Juvenile literature. I. Calvetti, Leonello. II. Massini, Luca. III. Title. IV. Series: Dalla Vecchia, Fabio Marco. Dinosaur profiles.

  QE862.S3D39 2004
  567.912—dc22   2004008696

CONTENTS

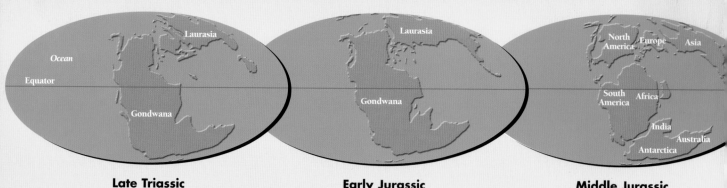

Late Triassic
227–206 million years ago

Early Jurassic
206–176 million years ago

Middle Jurassic
176–159 million years ago

A Changing World

Earth's long history began 4.6 billion years ago. Dinosaurs are some of the most fascinating animals from the planet's long past.

The word *dinosaur* comes from the word *dinosauria*. This word was invented by the English scientist Richard Owen in 1842. It comes from two Greek words, *deinos* and *sauros*. Together, these words mean "terrifying lizards."

The dinosaur era, also called the Mesozoic era, lasted from 248 million years ago to 65 million years ago. It is divided into three periods. The first, the Triassic period, lasted 42 million years. The second, the Jurassic period, lasted 61 million years. The third, the Cretaceous period, lasted 79 million years. Dinosaurs ruled the world for a huge time span of 160 million years.

Like dinosaurs, mammals appeared at the end of the Triassic period. During the time of dinosaurs, mammals were small animals the size

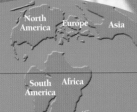

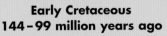

Late Jurassic	Early Cretaceous	Late Cretaceous
159–144 million years ago	**144–99 million years ago**	**99–65 million years ago**

of a mouse. Only after dinosaurs became extinct did mammals develop into the many forms that exist today. Humans never met Mesozoic dinosaurs. The dinosaurs were gone nearly 65 million years before humans appeared on Earth.

Dinosaurs changed in time. *Stegosaurus* and *Brachiosaurus* no longer existed when *Tyrannosaurus* and *Triceratops* appeared 75 million years later.

The dinosaur world was different from today's world. The climate was warmer, with few extremes. The position of the continents was different. Plants were constantly changing, and grass did not even exist.

A Terrifying Hunter

Deinonychus was a saurischian dinosaur of the group *Theropoda*. It was a small but skillful predator. Its most unusual feature was a large, sicklelike claw on each foot. It used these claws as weapons when it attacked its prey. In addition to the large claws on its feet, *Deinonychus* had three sharp claws on each hand. It also had seventy sharp teeth that were up to an inch (2.5 cm) long.

Deinonychus was the model for the fierce raptors in the movie *Jurassic Park*. In the movie, however, its size was doubled to make it look even more frightening. The real *Deinonychus* was about 10 feet (3 m) long and a little more than 3 feet (1 m) tall. It weighed about 100 pounds (45 kg). Its head was a foot (30 cm) in length. Compared with the size of its body, *Deinonychus's* brain was one of the largest of all the dinosaurs. *Deinonychus* was also more intelligent than many other dinosaurs. Its eyes were large and faced forward. This means it mainly used its sense of sight to find prey.

Deinonychus was bipedal, meaning it moved on two feet. It moved quickly, balancing its large head with a long, stiff tail.

Deinonychus lived during the Cretaceous period, 115 to 110 million years ago. Its remains have been found in Montana, Wyoming, Oklahoma, and possibly Utah. It lived along coastal plains of a sea that divided North America in two.

Although it was relatively small, *Deinonychus* could be very dangerous because of its pointed claws and sharp teeth.

This map shows North America as it was in the Early Cretaceous period. The dark brown area indicates mountains. The red dots indicate *Deinonychus* fossil discovery sites.

NORTH

AMERICA

Deinonychus Babies

A *Deinonychus* mother made its nest
out of sand. The nest was a shallow
hole with a raised rim like a bowl.

The mother laid two eggs at a
time in the center of the nest.
It could take several days to
produce as many as thirty
eggs. The mother sat on
the nest like a bird.

DEADLY SKILL

The young *Deinonychus* began to look for food by itself soon after hatching. The sicklelike claws on each foot were probably already developed. Its first prey were small animals living in the bushes or along the banks of streams. It would hunt for lizards, salamanders, or primitive mammals similar to mice. It patiently waited, then jumped on its prey, killing it with its big claws.

THE TRAP

Deinonychus was a very successful hunter. It was faster than most other dinosaurs and it was more nimble than a large carnivore. It probably hunted the large sauropods and ornithopods and the armored ankylosaurians. Some paleontologists think that *Deinonychus* hunted in packs because it was so much smaller than its prey. A young *Deinonychus* had the instinct to hunt as soon as it hatched, but it had to learn how to work with others in a pack.

No Escape

Deinonychus's favorite prey was a vegetarian dinosaur named *Tenontosaurus*. An adult tenontosaur was much larger than a *Deinonychus*. It was about 23 feet (7 m) long and weighed more than a half ton. Even though it was so big, it was in danger from small predators. It did not have claws to defend itself, and it could not run fast enough to escape a *Deinonychus*.

A *Deinonychus* pack attacked by kicking. They would kick the belly of their prey with the large claws on their feet. Then they would use their sharp teeth to rip large chunks of flesh from the victim. The tenontosaur could escape a single *Deinonychus*, but it could not survive the attack of a pack.

THE DEINONYCHUS BODY

The *Deinonychus* skull was large but light. It had wide openings for the eyes and for powerful jaw muscles.

Its teeth were curved and sharp. The back teeth had jagged edges to cut through flesh more easily.

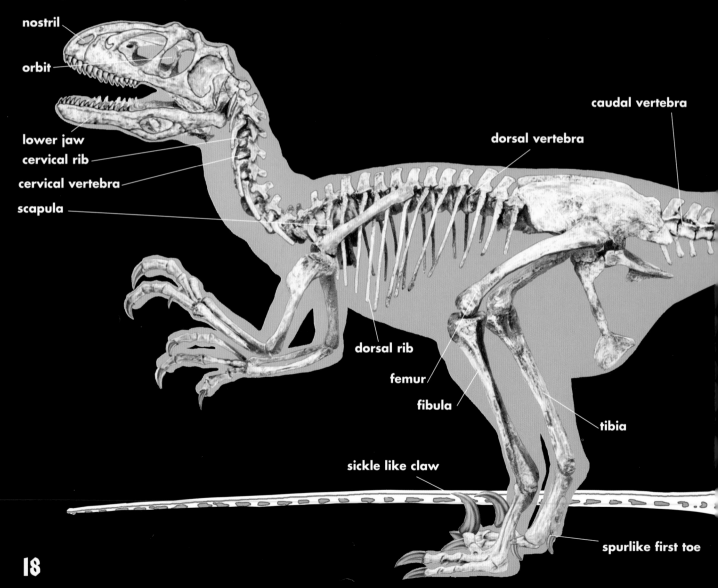

nostril

orbit

lower jaw

cervical rib

cervical vertebra

scapula

dorsal vertebra

caudal vertebra

dorsal rib

femur

fibula

tibia

sickle like claw

spurlike first toe

The left foot with the big claw

bony rods

Each foot had four toes, but only three were well developed. The toe with the large claw was short and strong. It was probably kept off the ground while the animal moved. From the footprints that *Deinonychus* left in the wet soil, it is clear that it walked on two toes, like an ostrich.

Its forearms were very long. Each hand had three thin fingers with long, sharp, hooked claws. They were used to hold prey that struggled to escape.

Deinonychus had a long tail that was kept stiff and straight by a layer of thin bony rods. Only the part of the tail closest to the body could be moved. The rest was rigid and straight like a broomstick. Besides *Deinonychus*, only primitive flying reptiles (pterosaurs) had this kind of tail.

claw on hand

sickle like claw on foot

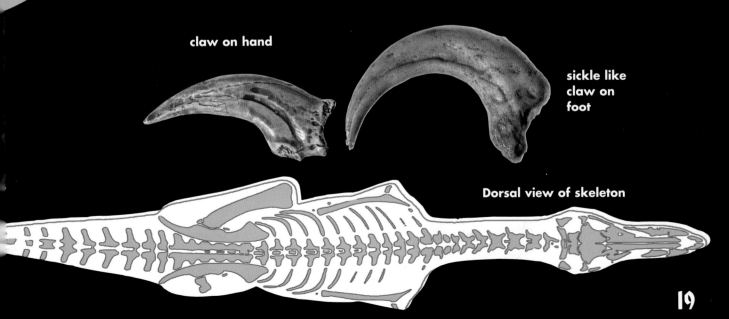

Dorsal view of skeleton

Digging Up Deinonychus

The first *Deinonychus* fossils were discovered in 1964 by paleontologists John Ostrom and Grant Meyer in the Bighorn Basin of southern Montana. The fossils were partial remains of three individuals found near the bones of a *Tenontosaurus*. In 1969 Ostrom named the fossil *Deinonychus*, from the Greek words for "terrible claw," because of the large claw on each foot. Other partial skeletons were discovered later, but never a complete one.

Deinonychus skeletons were light and delicate. Their bones were hollow and fragile. This made them less likely to last for millions of years, so *Deinonychus* fossils are rare. There are no completely preserved skeletons. Their teeth were solid, however, and had a better chance of being preserved. They are often the only fossil evidence of these animals.

The remains of a young *Deinonychus* and the bones of four tenontosaurs were recently discovered together in Oklahoma. This is evidence that *Deinonychus* preyed upon *Tenontosaurus*.

To date only ten partial skeletons of *Deinonychus* and several bones and teeth

This *Deinonychus* skeleton is on display at the Peabody Museum in Connecticut.

have been
discovered.
The only skeletal
model that has
original bones is
exhibited at the
American Museum of Natural History
in New York. The remains studied by
John Ostrom are at the Peabody
Museum at Yale University in New
Haven, Connecticut.

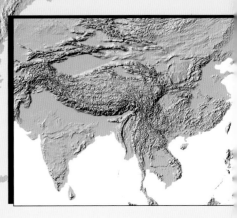

Many scientists believe that the Chicxulub crater off the coast of Mexico was made by a meteorite that led to the extinction of the dinosaurs.

● *Velociraptor,*
Mongolia,
80–70 million
years ago

● *Dromaeosaurus,*
Canada and USA,
78–65 million
years ago

Dromaeosaurus from Canada and the United States and the *Velociraptor* from Mongolia are close relatives of *Deinonychus*. They were smaller and lived million of years later, though. Dromaeosaurids with feathers have been found in China. Some paleontologists think dromaeosaurids are the dinosaurs most closely related to birds.

DROMAEOSAURIDS

● *Troodon, Canada and USA, 78–65 million years ago*

● *Deinonychus, USA, 115–110 million years ago*

THE GREAT EXTINCTION

Sixty-five million years ago, 50 million years after the time of *Deinonychus*, dinosaurs became extinct. This may have happened because a large meteorite struck Earth. A wide crater caused by a meteorite exactly 65 million years ago has been located along the coast of the Yucatán Peninsula in Mexico. The impact of the meteorite would have produced an enormous amount of dust. This dust would have stayed suspended in the atmosphere and blocked sunlight for a long time. A lack of sunlight would have caused a drastic drop of the earth's temperature and killed plants. The plant-eating dinosaurs would have died, starved and frozen. As a result, meat-eating dinosaurs would have had no prey and would also have starved.

Some scientists believe dinosaurs did not die out completely. They think that birds were feathered dinosaurs that survived the great extinction. That would make the present-day chicken and all of its feathered relatives descendants of the large dinosaurs.

THE EVOLUTION OF DINOSAURS

The oldest dinosaur fossils are 220–225 million years old and have been found mainly in South America. They have also been found in Africa, India, and North America. Dinosaurs probably evolved from small and nimble bipedal reptiles like the Triassic *Lagosuchus* of Argentina. Dinosaurs were able to rule the world because their legs were held directly under the body, like those of modern mammals. This made them faster and less clumsy than other reptiles.

Since 1887, dinosaurs have been divided into two groups based on the structure of their hips. Saurischian dinosaurs had hips shaped like those of modern lizards. Ornithischian dinosaurs had hips shaped like those of modern birds.

Triceratops is one of the Ornithischian dinosaurs, whose hip bones (inset) are shaped like those of modern birds.

There are two main groups of saurischians. One group is sauropodomorphs. This group includes sauropods, such as *Brachiosaurus*. Sauropods ate plants and were quadrupedal, meaning they walked on four legs. The other group of saurischians, theropods, includes bipedal meat-eating predators. Some paleontologists believe birds are a branch of theropod dinosaurs.

Ornithischians are all plant eaters. They are divided into three groups. Thyreophorans include the quadrupedal stegosaurians, including *Stegosaurus*, and ankylosaurians, including *Ankylosaurus*. The other two groups are ornithopods, which includes *Edmontosaurus* and marginocephalians.

25

A Dinosaur's Family Tree

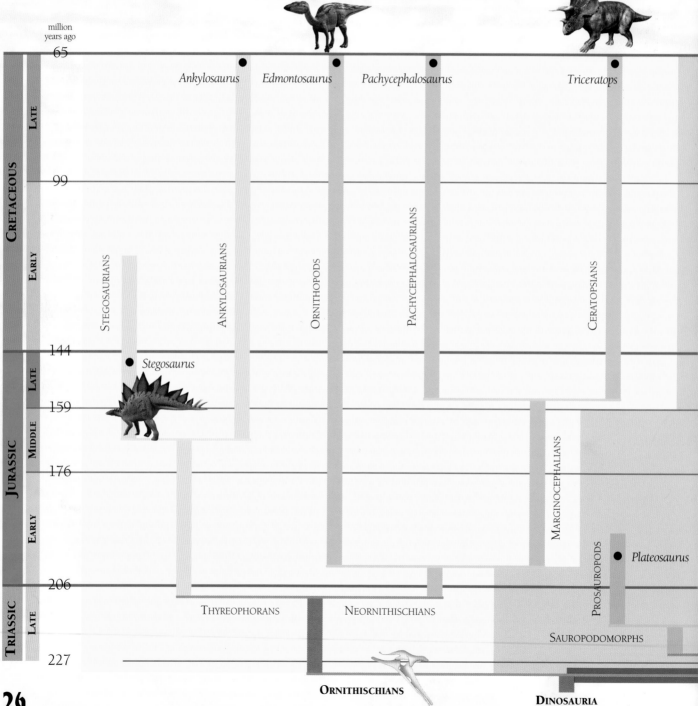

million years ago

65

99

144

159

176

206

227

CRETACEOUS — LATE, EARLY

JURASSIC — LATE, MIDDLE, EARLY

TRIASSIC — LATE

Ankylosaurus   *Edmontosaurus*   *Pachycephalosaurus*   *Triceratops*

STEGOSAURIANS   ANKYLOSAURIANS   ORNITHOPODS   PACHYCEPHALOSAURIANS   CERATOPSIANS

Stegosaurus

MARGINOCEPHALIANS

PROSAUROPODS

Plateosaurus

THYREOPHORANS   NEORNITHISCHIANS

SAUROPODOMORPHS

ORNITHISCHIANS

DINOSAURIA

Ornithomimus

Tyrannosaurus

ORNITHOMMOIDEANS

TYRANNOSAUROIDS

OVIRAPTOROSAURIANS

DEINONYCHOSAURIANS

BIRDS

Scipionyx

Deinonychus

SAUROPODS

ORNITHOLESTES

Caudipteryx

Brachiosaurus

THEROPODS

SAURISCHIANS

27

Glossary

Bipedal moving on two feet

Bone hard tissue made mainly of calcium phosphate

Carnivore meat eater

Caudal related to the tail

Cervical related to the neck

Claws sharp, pointed nails on the fingers and toes of predators

Cretaceous Period the period of geological time between 144 and 65 million years ago

Dorsal related to the back

Egg a large cell enclosed in a shell produced by reptiles and birds to reproduce themselves

Evolution changes in organisms over time

Feathers outgrowth of the skin of birds and some other dinosaurs, used for flight

Femur thigh bone

Fibula the outer of the two bones in the lower leg

Fossil a part of an organism of an earlier geologic age, such as a skeleton or leaf imprint, that has been preserved in the earth's crust

Jurassic Period the period of geological time between 206 and 144 million years ago

Mesozoic Era the period of geological time between 248 and 65 million years ago

Meteorite a piece of iron or rock that falls to Earth from space

Orbit the opening in the skull surrounding the eye

Pack group of predator animals hunting together

Paleontologist a scientist who studies prehistoric life

Paleozoic Era the period of geological time between 570 and 248 million years ago

Quadrupedal moving on four feet

Scapula shoulder blade

Scavenger animal that eats dead animals or plants

Skeleton the structure of an animal body, made up of bones

Skull the bones that form the cranium and the face

Tibia the shinbone

Triassic Period the period of geological time between 248 and 206 million years ago

Vertebrae the bones of the backbone

FOR MORE INFORMATION

Books

Paul M. Barrett, *National Geographic Dinosaurs*. Washington, DC: National Geographic Society, 2001.

Tim Haines, *Walking with Dinosaurs: A Natural History*. New York: Dorling Kindersley, 2000.

David Lambert, Darren Naish, and Elizabeth Wyse, *Dinosaur Encyclopedia: From Dinosaurs to the Dawn of Man*. New York: Dorling Kindersley, 2001.

Web Sites

The Cyberspace Museum of Natural History
www.cyberspacemuseum.com/dinohall.html
An online dinosaur museum that includes descriptions and illustrations.

Dinodata
www.dinodata.net
A site that includes detailed descriptions of fossils, illustrations, and news about dinosaur research and recent discoveries.

The Smithsonian National Museum of Natural History
www.nmnh.si.edu/paleo/dino
A virtual tour of the Smithsonian's National Museum of Natural History dinosaur exhibits.

ABOUT THE AUTHOR

Fabio Marco Dalla Vecchia is the curator of the Paleontological Museum of Monfalcone in Gorizia, Italy. He has participated in several paleontological field works in Italy and other countries and has directed paleontological excavations in Italy. He is the author of more than fifty scientific articles that have been published in national and international journals.

INDEX

Index